THE SEPTEMBER 11 ATTACKS
TRANSFORM AMERICA

BY WHITNEY SANDERSON

Published by The Child's World®
1980 Lookout Drive • Mankato, MN 56003-1705
800-599-READ • www.childsworld.com

ISBN 9781503825222
LCCN 2017959667

Printed in the United States of America
PA02376

ABOUT THE AUTHOR

Whitney Sanderson is the author of several children's historical fiction books.
She lives in western Massachusetts.

TABLE OF
CONTENTS

FAST FACTS

Who attacked the United States on September 11, 2001?

- Members of a terrorist group called al-Qaeda attacked the United States. The group was based in Central Asia. The leader of al-Qaeda was Osama bin Laden.

- Nineteen al-Qaeda **hijackers** boarded four planes in Boston, Massachusetts; Washington, DC; and Newark, New Jersey, on September 11. Soon after each flight left its airport, the hijackers took control of the planes.

What areas were attacked?

- The first two planes hit the Twin Towers of the World Trade Center in Lower Manhattan, New York City. The third plane hit the Pentagon building in Arlington County, Virginia. This building is the headquarters of the United States Department of Defense. People on the fourth plane resisted the hijackers. The plane crashed in a field in Shanksville, Pennsylvania.

TIMELINE

September 11, 2001, from 7:59 to 8:20 a.m.: Two American Airlines planes take off from Boston and Washington, DC. Each plane has five hijackers onboard.

September 11, 2001, from 8:14 to 8:42 a.m.: Two United Airlines planes take off from Boston and Newark with four to five hijackers on each plane.

September 11, 2001, from 8:46 to 9:03 a.m.: Planes crash into the World Trade Center's North Tower and South Tower.

September 11, 2001, at 9:05 a.m.: President George W. Bush is informed of the attacks.

September 11, 2001, at 9:37 a.m.: A plane hits the Pentagon.

September 11, 2001, at 9:59 a.m.: The South Tower collapses.

September 11, 2001, at 10:03 a.m.: A plane crashes in a field in Pennsylvania.

September 11, 2001, at 10:28 a.m.: The North Tower collapses.

Chapter 1

GROUND ZERO

Just after 8:00 a.m., Genelle Guzman-McMillan pushed open a door leading into a towering New York City skyscraper. She worked in the building, which was called the North Tower of the World Trade Center. She was an administrative assistant on the 64th floor. She grabbed her usual bagel and hot chocolate from a cafeteria in the building before heading to her desk.

It was a busy morning for Guzman-McMillan, with lots of calls to answer and paperwork to sign. A coworker, Susan Miszkowicz, stopped by to chat for a few minutes. While they were talking, a loud noise shook the building.

Guzman-McMillan thought it was an earthquake. She had experienced many of them in Trinidad, located in the Caribbean Sea, where she had grown up. The people around her began to panic. They ran to the windows, trying to see anything unusual outside. Papers and other **debris** floated gently from above. Another coworker, Rosa Gonzalez, said she thought a plane had hit the building.

A few minutes later, a supervisor ordered everyone to leave the building. Guzman-McMillan headed for the stairs with her coworkers. She could smell smoke. Then her ears were filled with a sound louder than a thousand earthquakes. "I felt the walls cave in. It was dark and everything was rumbling," said Guzman-McMillan.[1] She felt herself falling as the building collapsed around her.

She woke up in darkness. Her body was pinned by heavy metal beams. She was unable to move her head, arms, or legs. Only her left hand was free. It was in a pocket of air above her.

She called for help, but no one answered. She lay there for a long time, drifting in and out of consciousness. The air was filled with bitter-tasting ash.

On September 12, the site where the World Trade Center towers had stood was now called Ground Zero. Above the pile of rubble where Guzman-McMillan was trapped, a German Shepherd police dog named Trakr was picking his way among the piles of smoldering metal. Trakr's handler, a Canadian police officer named James Symington, followed the dog's lead. Trakr paused every few minutes to sniff an area with extra care. He stepped cautiously among the pieces of sharp metal and glass that littered the ground.

Trakr was taking part in the rescue efforts. He was trained to search disaster sites for survivors. But this 14.6-acre (6 ha) area, where fires still burned and dust filled the air, was his biggest challenge yet.

More than 16,000 people had been in the Twin Towers at the time of the first attack. Most people below the floors where the planes struck were able to get out before the towers fell. But thousands were still missing, along with hundreds of rescue workers who had gone into the buildings before the towers fell. By now, hope was fading that there were any more survivors.

Smoke spilled from the Twin Towers after planes crashed into ▶ them on September 11.

▲ Debris littered the streets after the towers collapsed.

Suddenly, Trakr gave Symington the signal for a hit. He had picked up the scent of someone trapped nearby. Guzman-McMillan opened her eyes. She thought she had heard someone. Then she felt a warm hand take hold of hers in the air pocket above. A comforting voice told her everything was going to be okay. A few minutes later, she saw a light shining. She felt the terrible weight of the fallen beams lift from her body. Soon she was being moved onto a stretcher and carried to an ambulance. She was the last person rescued from Ground Zero.

HELPING AFTER A DISASTER

First responders are people trained to help immediately after emergencies. The first responders on September 11 were firefighters, police officers, and emergency medical technicians. Later, helpers at Ground Zero included doctors, nurses, counselors, radio operators, construction workers, and volunteers.

Fires burned for 69 days in the World Trade Center wreckage.

An estimated 300 rescue dogs worked at Ground Zero.

Approximately 414 first responders were killed on September 11.

Approximately $9.5 billion of federal aid was given to New York within two months after September 11.

Chapter 2

A NATION MOURNS

When Steve McCurry heard about the September 11 attacks, his instinct was to grab his camera. He had been a professional photographer for more than 25 years. His photos had appeared on the cover of *National Geographic* and other magazines. He had traveled many times to take photographs in Middle Eastern countries.

That morning, McCurry was in his studio in Greenwich Village, New York. He had just returned from a trip to China. He hadn't even unpacked his equipment when he found out the World Trade Center towers were on fire.

McCurry looked out the window to see the Twin Towers in flames. He took photographs of the burning towers from his rooftop. After the towers fell, he decided to get closer. He knew that traffic and public transportation would be shut down. So he took his camera and headed toward the disaster on foot.

When McCurry arrived at Ground Zero, he found a scene of total chaos. Some people were trapped in the debris. Others surrounding the buildings had been hurt or killed when the towers collapsed. Many of them were firefighters and other first responders. Buildings, cars, and people were covered in ash. It looked like an eerie dusting of snow.

Hundreds of emergency workers had arrived from all over the city. They were caring for the wounded and searching for survivors. Everyone else had been ordered to leave the area, but some photographers and journalists stayed anyway. It wasn't long before nearby businesses and restaurants rallied to take food and supplies to the rescue workers.

13

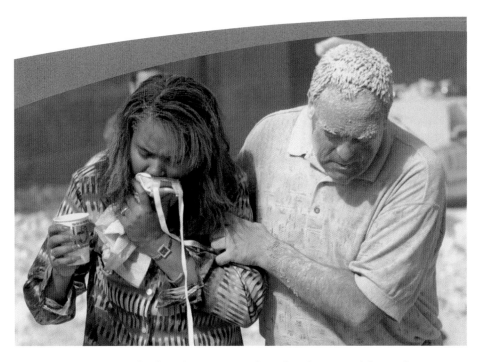

▲ Strangers helped one another in the World Trade Center attacks.

Although McCurry had taken photographs in war zones, it was still a shock to see such destruction on American soil. He tried to focus on his work. Through photographs, future generations could see details that would otherwise be forgotten. "It's something that you can't forget," McCurry said later. "I think my pictures tell that story of this epic destruction."[2]

McCurry was not surprised when al-Qaeda later claimed responsibility for the attacks. He had heard of this group before.

Toxins filled the air after the towers fell. Years later, ▶ more than 1,000 people who were near Ground Zero developed cancer.

They were feared and disliked by many of his Muslim friends. Al-Qaeda believed the United States was a land of greed and corruption. They also believed in *jihad*, a holy war to spread their beliefs.

In the weeks following September 11, McCurry visited **mosques** and Arab American centers across the city to take photographs. The people he met were filled with shock and sadness. Many mosques held memorial prayer services for the victims and their families and helped raise money for them.

Some Arab Americans were also afraid. They worried that some other Americans would not understand that their beliefs as Muslims were very different than those of the hijackers. Already, some people had experienced threats or even violence. McCurry hoped his photographs would help show people that Arab Americans were not different from other Americans. They had also lost friends and family in the attacks.

McCurry's photographs from September 11 captured a nation in mourning. In one picture, rescue workers and ambulances looked as tiny as ants among the blackened remains of the towers. In another, an American flag was planted in the middle of Ground Zero. It was a memorial for those who lost their lives and a symbol of hope for the future.

Steve McCurry captured the destruction at Ground Zero with ▶ his camera.

Chapter 3

THE WAR ON TERROR

President George W. Bush was sitting before a classroom full of students in Sarasota, Florida, when he heard the terrible news on September 11. The president's chief of staff, Andy Card, approached Bush quietly and whispered in his ear, "America is under attack."[3] Bush stayed outwardly calm to avoid frightening the children.

But his mind was racing. Later that evening, Bush addressed the nation on television. "America and our friends and allies join with all those who want peace and security in the world, and we stand together to win the war against terrorism," he said.[4]

But despite his words, Bush was concerned. His advisers warned him that fighting a war on terrorism was not like fighting an ordinary war. Many terrorists worked in small groups called cells. They were careful to hide their identities and leave no trace of their activities. When some of them were captured or killed, others were trained to take their places.

On October 7, 2001, Bush ordered the U.S. Army to invade Afghanistan in Central Asia. The army's mission was to remove the government party called the Taliban from power. The Taliban was known to support terrorist groups like al-Qaeda. While in Afghanistan, the army would also search for al-Qaeda leader Osama bin Laden and other terrorists involved in the September 11 attacks.

The war on terrorism continued for years. In March 2003, U.S. troops were sent to the Middle East. This time, they went into Iraq to overthrow its ruler, Saddam Hussein.

▲ In 2017, approximately 11,000 U.S. troops were in Afghanistan.

Although it later turned out not to be true, the U.S. government believed Saddam Hussein had **weapons of mass destruction.** Using these weapons was illegal under international law. Saddam Hussein was also a harsh ruler who often had his own people killed for disobeying laws.

Bush's plan was to create new governments where people could vote and choose their own leaders. He wanted to give people in these areas more opportunities for jobs and education.

Bush hoped that fewer young people would join terrorist groups like al-Qaeda. But keeping U.S. troops in the Middle East was extremely expensive, costing trillions of dollars per year. Thousands of American soldiers were killed while serving overseas.

Bush met the families of some of these soldiers. He visited a marine officer at the Walter Reed National Military Medical Center in Bethesda, Maryland. The marine had been badly injured in a bomb explosion. Bush presented him with a Purple Heart medal for courage, while the man's parents, wife, and five-year-old son watched. Bush remembered how the little boy's eyes had shone with pride for his father. The marine died in surgery six days later.

As the months and years went on, the idea of U.S. troops staying in Afghanistan and Iraq grew more unpopular in the United States. But now that America was involved, it seemed as though there was no easy way out. As of 2018, the war on terror continued with U.S. troops present in several countries, including Iraq, Afghanistan, and Syria.

Chapter 4

CHANGES AT HOME

At Logan International Airport in Boston, Massachusetts, people stood in a long line in front of a security checkpoint. Some of them nervously glanced at their watches, worried about missing their flights. Security agents carefully checked each person's boarding pass and identification. When people reached the front of the line, they had to remove their shoes, belts, and jewelry and walk past an X-ray machine.

Their luggage was also scanned with X-rays. Anything questionable was opened and inspected by security agents.

An agent in a uniform pulled one woman out of the lineup and asked her to throw a bottle of shampoo into a nearby trash can. The agent explained that the bottle was over the 3.4-ounce (100 mL) limit for liquids. A few minutes later, a man was taken aside. An agent swabbed his hands to check for traces of explosives. Nothing was found, so he was waved through. Nearby, a specially trained dog patrolled the airport with its handler. The dog was trained to detect the smell of drugs or explosives.

It was a typical scene at an airport after September 11. After the attacks, people criticized the airlines for not having enough security. The 19 hijackers had boarded the planes with box cutters and **mace** in their carry-on luggage. These weapons had allowed them to take control of the four planes.

After September 11, a new agency called the Transportation Security Administration took over security tasks in all U.S. airports. President Bush also passed other laws to help prevent future terror attacks. In October 2001, he signed the USA Patriot Act.

▲ Edward Snowden released secret government documents to the public in 2013. The documents showed how the government monitored people.

This new law allowed increased **surveillance** of citizens by the government. For example, it was now legal to monitor the e-mails, text messages, and phone calls of people suspected of terrorism. Some Americans thought this was a necessary step to keep people safe. Others were upset with the government.

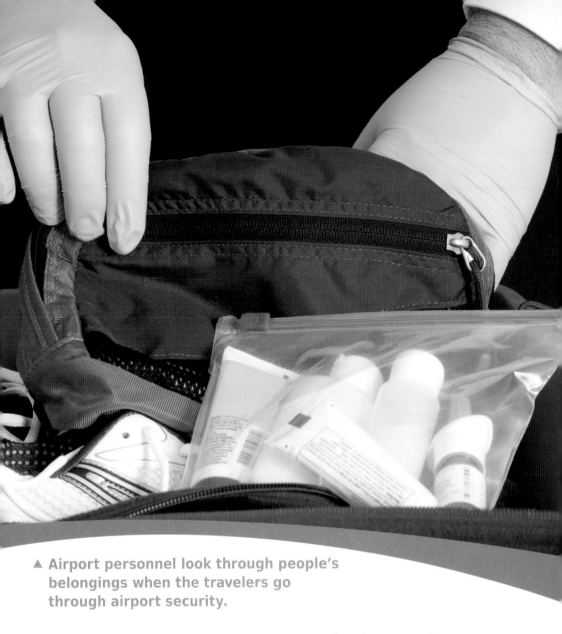

▲ Airport personnel look through people's
belongings when the travelers go
through airport security.

They thought it was an abuse of their **civil rights**. People
debated over the limits of the Patriot Act. The *New York Times*
reported on several cases where the Patriot Act was used to
monitor the communications of people suspected of crimes not
related to terrorism.

Chapter 5

NEW YORK REBUILDS

The sound of cheerful greetings echoed through the halls of New York City's P.S. 234 elementary school. Some kids lingered in the hallway to catch a few more seconds of conversation with friends, while others ran to classrooms to avoid being late.

In the classrooms, teachers welcomed back the students and took attendance. Colorful posters, maps, and children's drawings covered the classroom walls. It looked like an ordinary first day at an ordinary school. But for the students, parents, and teachers, it was a bittersweet return.

P.S. 234 was one of three schools near Ground Zero that had been evacuated during the September 11 attacks. The school had stayed closed for five months after the attacks due to air pollution from the debris and concerns about whether the neighborhood was safe. The students had been moved to schools farther away from Ground Zero.

Some parents questioned whether the school should reopen at all. Many of the children had frightening memories from September 11. Some had nightmares and drew pictures of burning buildings afterward.

But in the end, P.S. 234 opened its doors on February 4, 2002. Soon, old memories were replaced with new ones. Classmates who were separated were together again. For the students who had been there on September 11, their school was a symbol of survival and strength.

▲ The new World Trade Center tower is
1,776 feet (541 m) tall.

Months later, on May 30, 2002, the last steel beam from the
World Trade Center was removed from Ground Zero, draped in
an American flag. More than 108,000 truckloads of rubble had
been removed from the area.

In the years following the attack, a new 104-floor World Trade Center tower was built near the original site. It opened in November 2014. Some people who worked in the original Twin Towers returned to work there.

Today, Ground Zero is a park filled with trees and stone benches. Two square pools with waterfalls stand in the footprints of the original towers. The names of all the people who died on September 11 are written on bronze panels surrounding the pools. The memorial is open to the public. Every day, visitors come to the peaceful spot to rest, reflect, and remember.

THINK ABOUT IT

- What are some items or services that survivors and rescue workers might need after an event like September 11?
- If a disaster happened in your neighborhood, what could you do to contribute?
- Should the government have a right to listen to private calls or read e-mails of people who are suspected of terrorist activity? Explain your reasoning.

GLOSSARY

civil rights (SIV-il RITES): Civil rights are liberties that protect people's freedom and equal treatment. Some people believe the USA Patriot Act is a violation of their civil rights.

debris (duh-BREE): Pieces of broken and scattered material are known as debris. Debris from the World Trade Center filled streets after the September 11 attacks.

hijackers (HYE-jak-erz): Hijackers are people who take control of airplanes or other vehicles by force. Hijackers flew planes into buildings on September 11.

mace (MAYSS): Mace is a chemical spray that is irritating to the eyes and nose and can temporarily blind someone. Terrorists brought mace onto airplanes.

mosques (MOSKS): Places of Muslim worship are known as mosques. Many mosques in the United States held memorial prayer services after September 11.

surveillance (sur-VAY-luntz): Listening to or reading someone's private communication without their knowledge is known as surveillance. The USA Patriot Act increased the government's surveillance of citizens.

weapons of mass destruction (WEP-uhnz OV MASS di-STRUHK-shun): Weapons of mass destruction are weapons that can cause harm on a very large scale, such as bombs that use nuclear energy. The U.S. government believed Iraq had weapons of mass destruction.

SOURCE NOTES

1. "9/11 'Hero Dog' Saved Woman Trapped in Rubble for 27 Hours." *Today*. NBC Universal, 10 Sept. 2013. Web. 21 Dec. 2017.

2. "Interview with Steve McCurry on His 9/11 Photos." *YouTube*. YouTube, 24 July 2014. Web. 21 Dec. 2017.

3. "President George W. Bush: The 9/11 Interview." *YouTube*. YouTube, 11 Sept. 2011. Web. 21 Dec. 2017.

4. "Statement by the President in His Address to the Nation." *White House*. White House, 11 Sept. 2001. Web. 21 Dec. 2017.

TO LEARN MORE

Books

Goldish, Meish. *Ground Zero Dogs*. New York, NY: Bearport, 2013.

Haskell, L. S. *George W. Bush*. Mankato, MN: The Child's World, 2017.

Zullo, Allan. *Heroes of 9/11*. New York, NY: Scholastic, 2011.

Web Sites

Visit our Web site for links about September 11:

childsworld.com/links

Note to Parents, Teachers, and Librarians: We routinely verify our Web links to make sure they are safe and active sites. So encourage your readers to check them out!

INDEX